THE MILITARY ALLIANCE between the United States and South Korea "should continue forever," President Moon Jae-in declared in early November 2018. The South Korean leader said:

> *The Korea-U.S. alliance was forged in blood amid the artillery fire of the war, but it didn't stop there. It is developing into a great alliance that is creating peace on the Korean peninsula, drawing security and prosperity to the South and the U.S. and leading peace and stability in Northeast Asia.*

Judging from Seoul's official statements, the alliance, now spanning seven decades since the end of the fighting in the Korean War, appears to be strong. That is a matter of importance to every American because for more than a century U.S. policymakers have drawn their country's western defense perimeter not off the coast of California, or Hawaii, or Guam, but off the coast of East Asia. South Korea, on the tip of the Asian continent, anchors the northern end of that forward line of defense.

The loss of South Korea, therefore, would be grievous for America. Now, unfortunately, the relationship between the "blood allies" looks like it might not last much longer.

President Moon, despite his inspiring words, is working hard to end the pact. He first wants a "declaration of an end to the war" and then a treaty to formally bring the conflict to a close. His senior advisors, many of whom openly support Pyongyang, are on record saying there will be no need for American troops after peace is declared.

In the meantime, Moon has been conducting his own defense policies without consultation of his partner, the United States, sometimes taking actions that undermine the ability of Washington to defend South Korea. Moon's actions have predictably led some Americans to question whether the U.S. should remain on the peninsula.

Moon's highest priority is to reunify Korea – divided at the end of the Second World War – by merging the Republic of Korea, the South, and the Democratic People's Republic of

Korea, the North, even if that is accomplished on the North's terms. It is hard to imagine how Moon, known to have harbored anti-American views for decades, would want a U.S. presence on the peninsula after the two Koreas, ROK and DPRK, form a single state.

Moon's unification policy, unlike those of his predecessors, does not insist that a unified state be democratic as that term is understood in the South. As he works to unwind the alliance with the United States, Moon is also subverting the democracy he leads. He tried to amend the constitution to remove the concept of representative governance, and after that effort failed he went to work rewriting textbooks to remove references to liberty. He is jailing opponents and muzzling North Korean defectors while allowing pro-North thugs to work mischief and even break the law. He has orchestrated a climate of fear and intimidation.

The Republic of Korea is beginning to lose the badges of a free society. Moon, it appears, is trying to pave the way for unification by

The loss of South Korea would be grievous for America. Now, the relationship between the "blood allies" looks like it might not last much longer.

making South Korean society more compatible with the horrific regime in the North.

Most disturbingly, Moon Jae-in is enthusiastically taking down his country's defenses against North Korean infiltration and invasion and working to cripple the South Korean military. In short, he is making the South vulnerable. Some call him a "traitor." Only Moon himself truly knows his loyalties, yet if it were his intention to help Kim Jong Un, the North Korean despot, take over South Korea – if Moon were in fact a traitor – he would be doing exactly what he is doing now.

In consequence, the United States and the

free world are fast losing South Korea as an ally and partner.

THE ALLIANCE 'FORGED IN BLOOD'

"The era of no war has started," President Moon Jae-in announced in September 2018 during his summit with Kim Jong Un in Pyongyang. "Today the North and South decided to remove all threats that can cause war from the entire Korean peninsula."

In fact, an era of no war on the peninsula started in 1953, when Seoul and Washington signed the "alliance forged in blood." It is that alliance – and not pronouncements by a smiling Moon – that has kept the peace. The 1953 military pact inaugurated one of the more tranquil eras in all of Korean history.

Before then, the peninsula was a land of continuous conflict. There have been about nine hundred invasions and five major occupations of Korea over the millennia. It took Japan's defeat in World War II to end the last of those occupations. Korea technically did not exist as a country during the fighting.

Although Japanese troops went home in defeat, Korea turned out to be the global conflict's big loser. The Cairo Declaration of 1943 stated that "in due course, Korea shall become free and independent," but events seemed to conspire against the Korean people, and so did the allies. In seeking help for the fight against Japan, President Truman persuaded the Soviet Union to declare war on Tokyo, which it finally did on August 8, 1945 – just seven days before the emperor capitulated. The U.S. government, determined to prevent a Soviet occupation of Japan, permitted Moscow to enter Korea. The Red Army crossed into the northern part of the peninsula the next day, August 9.

Washington had given almost no thought to the question of what to do with Korea, and no U.S. forces were there. In order to avoid a Soviet occupation of the entire peninsula, America proposed that Korea be divided. Two days after Soviet troops entered Korea, two junior U.S. Army officers, after glancing at a

National Geographic map, picked the 38th parallel as the border for "temporary" occupation zones. Lieutenant Colonel Dean Rusk, later to become secretary of state, and his colleague unknowingly selected a line that had significance in Korean history and thereby inadvertently signaled to Moscow that the United States recognized the tsar's old claim to the northern portion of the peninsula. The Soviets accepted and honored the proposed boundary. Korea, which had been unified for more than a millennium, was severed in two.

In different times, there might have been no consequence to the last-minute decision to split the peninsula, but in the ensuing competition between Moscow and Washington the stopgap measure took on lasting significance. There were supposed to be national elections in Korea, sponsored by the United Nations, but they were never held, and eventually each side in the global rivalry established its own client state. The American-backed Republic of Korea was officially established on August 15, 1948, and the Soviet-supported Democratic People's Republic of Korea was proclaimed less than a month later.

This arrangement was unstable from the beginning. Each of the two states claimed to be the sole representative of the Korean people. Both were looking for a military solution, and neither of the big-power sponsors stayed around to ensure order. Soviet troops left by late 1948, and the Americans were gone by June 1949. The North and South were left to settle their fate by force of arms.

Both sides conducted guerilla raids and battalion-size incursions across the dividing parallel. When Kim Il Sung, the founder and leader of North Korea, sent tanks and troops south on June 25, 1950, Truman intervened immediately. The United Nations, prompted by Washington, joined the fight.

America, however, did not have the resolve to win. After armies marched up and down the peninsula in what was called the "accordion war," Washington accepted a truce, roughly along the 38th parallel, in July 1953.

This time, American forces did not leave, and a formal alliance was signed between Washington and Seoul months after the truce.

It is this alliance that today allows Moon to feel secure enough to reach out to Pyongyang. Yet he appears intent on undermining the pact. For instance, the president has allowed senior aides to try to turn public opinion against the arrangement by mischaracterizing the command structure of alliance forces. Moon's officials, beginning soon after his inauguration in May 2017, publicly complained that a U.S. general would command South Korean troops in the event of a North Korean attack.

That claim was not true, as David Maxwell, who served five tours of duty with the U.S. Army in South Korea, explained at the time:

> *President Moon's advisors know full well the U.S. does not have command of ROK forces. The Moon administration should explain the nature of the command relationship to the Korean people and inform them that the ROK president has*

equal authority and control over the ROK/U.S. Combined Forces Command. The Military Committee ensures equal authority and control over the combined command, and it is time for the ROK leadership to both state that in public and take equal responsibility for the combined command and the defense of the ROK.

Moon has been making other moves to weaken the South's defenses. In the summer and fall of 2018, the president unilaterally authorized the taking down of barbed-wire fencing and observation posts in the Demilitarized Zone, the 160-mile-long strip separating the two Koreas. He also ordered the demolition of tank traps, meant to slow North Korean armor racing to the South Korean capital. He proposed to cut the number of army divisions significantly and to reduce the period of conscription from twenty-one months to eighteen. As Tara O of the Pacific Forum told me, "Moon is not only leaving the door open, he's removing all the doors and windows."

Analysts are also concerned about the seventeen-page military agreement inked in September 2018 with Kim Jong Un during Moon's visit to Pyongyang. Ms. O noted, for instance, that the deal's enlargement of the no-fly zone over the DMZ and border waters reduces the South's warning time in the event of an attack. Experts are also worried about the withdrawal of South Korean artillery from islands in the Yellow Sea, or West Sea as both Koreas call it.

The central problem with the September agreement is that it helps the attacker far more than the defender. Some South Koreans called it a "surrender document" because it looked like Moon was attempting to abandon the defense of the Republic of Korea.

Moon has also been undermining the defense of his homeland in more insidious ways, such as in dealings with China. For a good part of this decade, Beijing was pressuring Seoul to prevent the deployment in South Korea of the Terminal High Altitude Area Defense system, designed to shoot down missiles. When the campaign to stop THAAD failed, the Chinese retaliated. Beijing targeted the Lotte Group and other South Korean businesses in China, blocked imports from the South, and limited the number of Chinese citizens visiting there. Beijing's leaders were angry that Seoul ignored its concerns that THAAD radar could look into Chinese airspace.

Even if THAAD radar could do that, Beijing's campaign was particularly bold because the system blocked a threat that China had helped create. Beijing had supplied crucial equipment and probably highly advanced technology to the Kim family's ballistic missile program and had also allowed Chinese enterprises to supply components, equipment, and materials to the regime's nuclear weapons initiative.

Moon, however, sided with Beijing in the dispute. At the end of October 2017, he issued the now-infamous "Three Nos": no to the hosting of additional THAAD batteries, no to participating in an integrated missile defense system with the United States, and no to joining an alliance with Japan and the U.S. These three negative commitments undermined an effective defense of the Republic of Korea and limited "U.S. political-military action without any apparent or known consultation with Washington," as David Maxwell put it.

In short, Moon's accommodation with Beijing, called a capitulation to "Chinese bullying" by the conservative *Chosun Ilbo* newspaper, was inconsistent with the alliance with America. Since then, Washington has been loath to criticize Moon in public for fear of rupturing relations, but there is not much cooperation. The pact that has kept the peace on the peninsula since July 1953 might not last the decade.

FLAGS OF THE ENEMY

Moon Jae-in puts trust not in the alliance with America but in friendship with his country's enemy. And he sometimes shows more allegiance to that enemy than to the state he was elected to lead.

When Moon arrived in Pyongyang in September 2018, a reported 100,000 people greeted him, many waving either the North Korean flag or the blue-and-white Korean unification standard. No one was holding the symbol of Moon's country, the Republic of Korea, yet he smiled the whole time and showed no displeasure at this breach of diplomatic protocol. The only South Korean flags in evidence were the two painted on the plane that brought Moon to Pyongyang and the flag badge on the lapel of Samsung's Lee Jae-yong. None of Moon's aides wore a lapel badge of the South's flag. Moon didn't either.

Throughout the trip, Moon went out of his way to downplay the legitimacy of the country he was elected to represent. His language was the key sign. While visiting the North, he often referred to South Korea as "*nam cheuk*," literally meaning "south side" or "south," when the custom has been for South Korean leaders to say "*Hanguk*," literally "country of Han people." Moon also spoke of "*nam cheuk gookmin*," which translates as "southside citizens." South Korean presidents would normally say "*uri gookmin*," literally "our citizens" and figuratively "my citizens." In effect,

---

Moon Jae-in's highest priority is to reunify Korea, even if that is accomplished on the North's terms.

Moon's terminology portrayed South Koreans as residents of one geographical part of Korea rather than the citizens of a distinct country.

Kim Jong Un did not reciprocate Moon's rhetorical gestures. During Moon's visit, Kim used the communist term "*uri inmin*," meaning "our people" or "my people." Kim showed no reluctance conveying the notion that North Korea was a fully legitimate country.

Neither of the Korean states – Moon's Republic of Korea or Kim's Democratic People's Republic of Korea – recognizes the other as legitimate. Moon's choice of terms during the visit was a subtle but significant signal that he was not even asserting the legitimacy of his own country.

Moon looks like he wants to change Seoul's core position with respect to Korean political legitimacy. Since the founding of the South Korean state, school textbooks have stated that Seoul is "the only legitimate government on the Korean peninsula." Moon's Ministry of Education, disturbingly, has already changed textbooks to eliminate that foundational declaration. In addition, as reported by Tara O, also a former U. S. Air Force intelligence analyst, the South's Unification Ministry has deleted the critical phrase from training materials.

Since the division of Korea in 1945, every Korean leader, both north and south of the Demilitarized Zone, has advocated unification. It's no surprise then that Moon, in his summits with Kim, has promoted the union of the two rival Koreas. The Pyongyang Declaration of September 19, 2018, issued by Moon and Kim during their summit in the North Korean capital, states:

The two leaders reaffirmed the principle of independence and self-determination of the Korean nation, and agreed to consistently and continuously develop inter-Korean relations for national reconciliation and cooperation, and firm peace and co-prosperity, and to make efforts to realize through policy measures the aspiration and hope of all Koreans that the current developments in inter-Korean relations will lead to reunification.

Over the years, both Seoul and Pyongyang have put forward unification schemes, like the "Democratic Confederal Republic of Koryo" proposed by Kim Il Sung and the "Korean Commonwealth" or "Korean National Community" advanced by President Roh Tae Woo of South Korea. Most of these proposals have contemplated one state with two separate governments as an interim step toward full union, but even these loose arrangements failed to gain the necessary support. The two Korean states have proved so different and so hostile that a "marriage of equals" has never been implemented.

Implementation could occur soon, however. Moon looks like the first Korean leader to accept unification on the terms of the other state. To pave the way for union, he has been trying to make South Korea's form of government more compatible with the North's.

Most fundamentally, Moon's Democratic Party of Korea in early 2018 led an attempt to remove the notion of "liberal" from the concept of "democratic" in the country's constitution. The South's "conservatives" turned back the effort, but the Education Ministry in June of that year proposed to change the country's textbooks to describe the nation's political system as just "democracy," rather than "free democracy." The ministry ultimately succeeded in removing references to "freedom" from middle-school textbooks.

On the Korean peninsula, democracy does not have to be "liberal." The Kimist regime rejects the concept of liberalism but nonetheless maintains that it is "democratic." Its formal name, after all, is the Democratic People's Republic of Korea. Moon's political party shares the "Democratic" label but is leading the attack on liberal governance.

Moon is clearly eroding democratic institutions in South Korea. Since becoming president, he has exercised control of big broadcasters to reduce the airing of dissenting views and to promote the North Korean perspective. "An American expert recently visiting Korea was warned by a state-funded media outlet to avoid any remarks critical of Moon's approach to North Korea," a leading authority on pro–North Korea activities, Lawrence Peck, told me in September 2018.

To reinforce its control over messaging, Moon's government has also clamped down on social media. The Justice Ministry has been thinking of ways it can remove content judged to be causing "social distrust."

Minjoo, as the president's party is known, is sponsoring a "broadcast law reform" bill, which if enacted will give the government the right to remove YouTube videos from circulation. "YouTube remains the only open venue for those Koreans who want to safeguard their country as a democratic republic," writes In-ho Lee, a former South Korean diplomat and once president of the Korea Foundation.

Moon has demonstrated that he does not need a law to pressure YouTube. His administration began an investigation of Google Korea for tax evasion after the company refused a request from the ruling party to take down 104 YouTube videos. Minjoo Party members, perhaps as retribution, have threatened to impose regulation on social media. Moon's government has announced it is preparing to impose sanctions on material considered damaging to society.

In his campaign to suppress dissent, Moon has been nothing if not relentless. The National Police Agency has been investigating stories that his administration has deemed to be factually incorrect.

An often-used tactic has been, as Peck explains, the bringing of "extremely dubious criminal defamation charges against critics." Some of those critics are journalists. Perhaps the most significant prosecution of a journalist is that of Byun Hee-jai of Mediawatch. In December 2018, Byun and three Mediawatch colleagues were found guilty of libeling JTBC, a cable TV channel, when they questioned the accuracy of its story about a tablet computer that was instrumental in the impeachment and removal from office of Moon's predecessor, Park Geun-hye. An acquittal of Byun and the other journalists would have been tantamount to an admission that the JTBC story was inaccurate. That, Tara O explained to me, would have raised "the question why Park was impeached in the first place." Given the unusual circumstances of the case – prosecutions of libel are rare and pre-conviction detention rarer still – there is almost certainly a political element to the decision to convict Byun and his colleagues.

Moon's government has also sought to silence other critics. For instance, in an attempt to promote reconciliation with Pyongyang, the administration has been pressuring North Korean defectors who have found refuge in the South to keep quiet about the Kim regime.

Moreover, Moon's administration compiled various "blacklists" of citizens targeted for surveillance and harassment.

In short, conservative voices are, in the words of Peck, being "persecuted, censored, fired, prosecuted, pressured, or otherwise retaliated against or harassed."

The result is what In-ho Lee, the former diplomat, calls a "reign of terror." The intimidation campaign started off as "imperceptible," and even today it is marked more by what is not seen or heard than what is. "Now, no one talks politics," Lee said in November 2018. "That's the reign of terror."

Silence is perhaps the most significant symptom of Moon's repression. Another

---

Kim Jong Un wants to take over the South, and Moon Jae-in looks like he is trying to help him do it.

---

symptom is South Korea's isolation. A prominent American Korea analyst told me, also in November, that some of her friends in the South do not want her to contact them anymore as they are fearful of being hounded by Moon's administration for talking to an American critic of the government.

Fear of the government is noticeable in other ways too. At the anti-Moon "Taegukgi" rallies in Seoul, many young demonstrators feel compelled to wear masks or otherwise hide their faces from photographers.

There is reason for South Koreans to be concerned because dangerous elements now, as a practical matter, have license to do what they want. Pro–North Korea forces in the South feel free not only to speak but also to act, and to deny freedom to others. The North's radical proponents hold rallies in which they demand the arrest of "scum," as they characterize those who have escaped the North to live in the South. Radicals put up wanted posters in Seoul naming two defectors and asking residents to report their whereabouts. Because the two are believed to be targeted by Pyongyang for assassination, the posters put their lives in danger.

The now-notorious Baekdu Group, pro-North activists, and affiliates such as the "Flower Wave" have broken into classrooms to shout propaganda; into the offices of the Daily NK, a web-based news organization, to intimidate staff; and into the offices of a human rights organization to disrupt its operations. Baekdu Group members have made public death threats and staged mock public arrests with victims bound in rope, suggesting lynching. They have scuffled with police.

Some South Koreans believe that "free democracy" in their country is "currently on the verge of a collapse," as it was put in the "Statement of the Congress of the Republic of Korea on the National Emergency on the Situations That Face the Nation," published on September 4, 2018. Alarm over the loss of freedom is now widespread in South Korea.

Of course, Moon did not invent South Korean authoritarianism. The country has a long history of hardline rule, starting with its first leader, Syngman Rhee, and continuing with strongman Park Chung Hee and two generals-turned-presidents, Chun Doo Hwan and Roh Tae Woo. Park Geun-hye and her post-Roh predecessors also used – and abused – the power of the state.

Moon promised to be different. In his inauguration speech in May 2017, he declared, "I will strive to get rid of authoritarian practices in the presidency." Although he made his name as a human rights lawyer and campaigner for democracy, Moon has been far more aggressive in the use of state power than his predecessor, Park. He has reversed a decades-long trend of democratization and liberalization and is now returning the South to a dark period. The South Korea of tomorrow, unfortunately, could resemble the South Korea of the past.

A 'New Korea'

"I take the first step toward a new Korea," Moon declared at his inauguration. And he has promised that something else will be new. "A new order is being created on the Korean peninsula," he proclaimed in October 2018.

A new order is precisely what worries many segments of South Korean society. If Moon gets his way, there will almost certainly be a formal union with the DPRK, and the union would almost certainly be a confederal republic. If so, such a republic would have two parallel governments.

Kim Il Sung proposed a confederation as only a waystation to a full takeover of the southern government. As David Maxwell, the former Army officer who is now at the Foundation for Defense of Democracies, points out, the Kim family has never abandoned its overarching goal of ruling the entire peninsula from Pyongyang. Therefore, Kim rulers have employed, and continue to employ, "subversion, coercion, extortion, and use of force." Within a formal union, Kim Jong Un would have more opportunities to subvert, coerce, extort, and force the southern government into submission – especially with someone like Moon, a sympathizer, who would not be inclined to defend the institutions of his society.

Nor would Moon's closest advisors be so inclined. His inner circle includes those who, as members of the so-called *juchesasangpa* groups, advocated North Korea's *juche* self-reliance ideology; in other words, they worked for a takeover of the South by the North. To this day, some of them have refused to disavow their youthful views. Concerns swirled around Im Jong-seok, Moon's radical chief of staff, until he was forced out in early January 2019. Moreover, Moon has continued to hire far-left figures as advisors.

The danger for freedom-loving South Koreans, whether or not there is a formal union, is that there is now congruence between the general aims and objectives of the Kim family ruling the North and those of Moon and his advisors governing the South.

Does this mean South Korea's liberal institutions are doomed? There are several reasons to think they are not. First, despite all the unification talk, it is not clear that Moon's pro–North Korea advisors actually desire a takeover of the South by the North. As Maxwell told me, the "*juche* faction" wants, most of all, "personal political power."

Personal political power for them, at least over an extended period, would not be possible in a Kimist regime. North Korea is the closest thing to a one-man state in the world today. Everything in Kim Jong Un's "government," if it could be called that, has been structured to enhance and ensure the continued rule of the Kim family, including a suffocating cult of personality. Kim Il Sung was ruthless in eliminating any independent power centers, and so was his son and successor, Kim Jong Il. Kim Jong Un, Kim Jong Il's son and successor, has been particularly bloodthirsty, executing hundreds of officials as soon as he unexpectedly inherited power at the end of 2011.

As Maxwell notes, Moon's officials have no interest in being "absorbed" by Kim. Because personal position is probably more important to Moon's officials than ideology, the existence of two Korean states – or at least two Korean governments in a unified state – for the foreseeable future seems probable.

Second, Moon Jae-in, whatever his intentions, may not have the political leverage to accomplish his objectives. In short, he is losing popularity fast. South Korean presidents, more than other democratically elected leaders, suffer this fate, in part because they are permitted only one term and are therefore lame ducks from the moment they are sworn in.

Defying the familiar pattern, Moon remained popular for more than a year after taking office. He gained popularity largely because of his outreach to Kim Jong Un, earning an 86 percent approval rating, the highest for a South Korean president ever, in the wake of his first summit with his North Korean counterpart. But then began a relentless across-the-board decline in approval among all regional and ideological segments and all age brackets of the population.

Moon's high-handedness and top-down

style are not especially appealing. Even his most fervent supporters have chafed under his leadership. At the end of 2018, students in more than a hundred universities across the country posted notices calling him "King Moon." His primary problem, however, is that he has devoted most of his energies to North Korean relations while the electorate has been most concerned about pocketbook issues. And Moon has been plagued by the perception that he has persistently mismanaged the economy.

The popularity of the self-proclaimed "jobs president" fell under the 50 percent line for the first time in September 2018, especially due to anger over weak employment numbers, the worst job growth in almost nine years. His left-leaning policies – he is called a "socialist" in some quarters for his "income-led growth" approach – have failed to perk up the economy. "We treat this situation gravely," said Kim Eui-keum, Moon's spokesman, reacting to the drop in public favor. Although Moon promised to "pay more attention to the voice of the people," his approval numbers have continued to decline, perhaps because "the people" he has been trying to please, his radical base, favor policies that tend to stunt growth. Moon's "J-nomics" has been a bust and so have recent attempts to move toward more centrist policies, which have alienated "progressive," including far-left, supporters.

Moon has apparently thought that one way out of his economic predicament is to take advantage of the inexpensive labor pool just north of the Demilitarized Zone. His "New Korean Peninsula Economic Map," which calls for joint manufacturing zones and the reopening of the Kaesong Industrial Complex, could be, as one observer put it, his "saving grace." In his annual Liberation Day speech in August 2018, Moon proposed "a single economic community" for the two Koreas.

Most of what Moon would like to do, however, is prohibited by UN Security Council or U.S. sanctions. There is a limit, therefore, on what he can achieve through economic cooperation with Kim's Korea at this time.

For the foreseeable future, the economy will weigh on Moon's closely watched popularity ratings.

Third, unification is not as popular as it might first appear. Decades ago, reuniting the peninsula had broad and deep support in the South. But then South Koreans witnessed the costs of unification borne by West Germans and decided that although unification

Moon puts trust not in the alliance with America but in friendship with his country's enemy. And he sometimes shows more allegiance to that enemy than to the state he was elected to lead.

remained a goal, it should be postponed until the gap between the two Koreas had been narrowed.

Since the beginning of the 1990s, the estimated cost of Korea's unification has varied from about $600 billion to $5 trillion, with estimates rising over time. When President Roh Tae Woo said in 1991 that "our people do not want accelerated unification," he was telling the truth. Since the early 1990s, in truth, the cost has always been thought to be too high.

This general attitude, bordering on selfishness, has limited what Moon can do to support the Kim regime, especially at a time when his own economy is ailing. Moreover, there are broad segments of the South Korean electorate, the oldest and the youngest, that are generally skeptical of his outreach to the North.

Older voters remember the June 1950 invasion by North Korea and harbor unshakably unfavorable views of the Kim regime. Moon's attempts at bridge-building with the current Kim, such as removal of textbook references to the invasion of the South, are particularly unwelcome in the top age cohorts.

Younger voters do not appear to buy into Moon's unificationist stance either. Many of them do not see their country as "Korea," instead identifying themselves as South Koreans. They perceive the North as a nuclear threat, a destitute state, and a belligerent neighbor. The North Koreans are, in a word, foreigners. In a poll conducted in 2017 by the Korea Institute for National Unification, only 38.9 percent of respondents in their twenties favored unification.

That same survey found relatively high support for unification in society as a whole, with 57.8 percent favoring it. Yet the push for union with the North has been faltering. A survey in 2014 had found 69.3 percent favoring a merging of the two Koreas.

Moon himself has lost appeal at times when the South Korean public believes that his unification policies have overreached, as in early 2018 when he forced the addition of

North Korean players to the South's women's ice hockey team for the PyeongChang Winter Olympics in South Korea. His approval dropped to a four-month low in January 2018 – down six percentage points in a week – due to resentment over this overbearing maneuver. Some polls showed a ten-point fall in two weeks. Few liked the idea that South Korean athletes were turfed off their own team for political reasons, and the Games were widely mocked as "the Pyongyang Olympics." Younger South Koreans showed higher levels of disapproval in surveys.

This new nationalism in South Korea – not Korean nationalism but South Korean nationalism – undercuts the popularity of unification projects. As a result, Moon has only one realistic option for regaining popularity.

"This is not a country where logic prevails," the late Usung Chung, a South Korean who maintained the provocative Eyes on Korea blog, told me in the middle of the last decade. "You have to appeal to the emotion. And that emotion changes so wildly."

Moon's best hope to rebuild his political base requires a wild change in public emotion in favor of Kim Jong Un. With Moon's help, in fact, Kim has won South Korean hearts. And Kim has helped himself too. His finger-heart gesture, made with South Korean officials in September 2018, went viral south of the Demilitarized Zone.

So Kim can help Moon, but the South Korean president needs Kim's cooperation. A Kim visit to the South's capital is bound to trigger optimism, even euphoria, and high poll numbers for the South Korean president. The Pyongyang Declaration of September 2018 states that the North Korean leader "agreed to visit Seoul at an early date."

Moon went on the record as saying that Kim promised to come to Seoul sometime in 2018. Many thought the historic trip would occur in November, and when Kim failed to show then the betting was December. Moon worked hard to arrange a December visit. It appears he orchestrated the formation of pro-visit groups, block-booked hotel rooms in Seoul for North Korean officials, and stoked media speculation with hopeful comments. Despite all the activity, Kim had not shown by the end of 2018.

Now, the Moon administration hopes Kim will make the visit in 2019. The visit, if it occurs, will be historic. No North Korean leader has set foot in the South Korean capital since the end of the fighting in the Korean War. Kim Jong Un, when he stepped over the Military Demarcation Line in Panmunjom in late April 2018, was in fact the first Kim ruler to go to South Korea in peacetime.

Kim's father, Kim Jong Il, also promised to go to Seoul but never did, and Moon will lose popularity if the current leader does not honor his promise soon. That's especially true because Kim has so far been quite the traveler. He made his first trips abroad as leader in 2018, including three to China: to Beijing at the end of March, his first visit outside his regime; in the beginning of May to Dalian;

and again in June to Beijing, following his summit with President Trump. Kim then took the train to Beijing in January 2019. Four successive trips to China – while the Chinese ruler Xi Jinping has yet to go to the DPRK – makes it look like Kim was summoned by the Chinese.

Moon, unfortunately for him, has no such pull with Kim, and so he has essentially put his political future, not to mention his legacy, in the North Korean's hands. If Kim is fundamentally different from his two predecessors and is determined to enter the international community, Moon will be extraordinarily successful. If Kim remains outside the community of nations, however, Moon's legacy will be tarnished like those of his two "progressive" predecessors, Kim Dae Jung and Roh Moo-hyun.

After taking office in 1998, D.J., as Kim Dae Jung was known, immediately promoted his Sunshine Policy, named after the Aesop fable in which the Sun is able to persuade a man to take off his coat after the North Wind fails to do so. "We will actively push reconciliation and cooperation between the South and North beginning with those areas which can be most easily agreed upon," Kim announced in his inaugural address.

Kim Jong Il did not respond well to the other Kim's overtures even though the South's policies were unusually generous. The soft South Korean approach did not decrease military tensions, for example. On the contrary, the unappeasable DPRK even increased its infiltrations and incursions. Pyongyang just took Seoul's cash, which D.J. was happy to supply, and continued developing ballistic missiles and nuclear weapons. Sunshine, which was not working, stopped being a policy and became an end in itself.

Eventually, the South Korean public lost patience. They became "sunburnt," said Park Jin, then a leading opposition figure in South Korea's national legislature. Too much sunshine created a desert, observed Norbert Vollertsen, a North Korea activist.

The apparent failure of Sunshine did not

deter D.J.'s successor. Roh Moo-hyun sought to fix the policy – by changing its label. Seoul in the Roh era talked about a Peace and Prosperity Policy as if it were different, but it was, in reality, the Sunshine approach. When the North Koreans refused to cooperate, Roh lost his standing in the South and earned the nickname "Roh the idiot."

All of this should serve as a lesson for Moon because, among other things, he was Roh's chief of staff. Now, Moon risks the same fate as his old boss.

THE NUCLEAR CRISIS

Moon Jae-in's main problem now is that he is caught in the middle. Kim Jong Un has shown little desire to give up his most destructive weapons, and Donald John Trump has continued to press him to do so. Among other things, the Washington-Pyongyang confrontation creates even more frustration for the South Korean president.

South Koreans have often likened their nation to a "shrimp among whales." Roh Moo-

> *Kim has been talking about "final victory." Now, for the first time since the early days of the Korean War, that looks possible, perhaps even probable.*

hyun did not buy the shrimp analogy, however. Exhibiting the extraordinary cockiness of his times, he believed that Seoul should play a "balancing role," switching sides on an issue-by-issue basis between the "northern alliance" of Beijing, Moscow, and Pyongyang on the one side, and the "southern alliance" of Washington and Tokyo on the other. "The power equation in Northeast Asia will change depending on the choices we make," he said.

Moon, more diplomatic than his old boss, is not that explicit, but Roh's statement sums up much of the current president's thinking. Moon has in fact steered a middle course between the Americans and the Chinese, something evident from the issuance of the "Three Nos," and a middle course between the Americans and the North Koreans.

For Moon, Kim's nuclear weapons program is only an obstacle to the unification of the two Koreas. So far, the South Korean president, who has made an "irreversible 'all-in' bet" on North Korea as with his other policies, is getting his way. In September 2018, over U.S. objections, Moon opened a liaison office in the now-closed Kaesong Industrial Complex, which is just north of the DMZ. Both the establishment of the office and Seoul's supply of electricity to the zone are violations of UN sanctions.

To keep the alliance intact, Washington has acceded to most of Moon's initiatives and has avoided public criticism, and so far the situation is manageable as both Washington and Seoul, to varying degrees, are trying to engage Pyongyang. Yet this congruence is unlikely to last long. Trump administration policy is bound to take a turn that will widen the gap.

Through about the middle of May 2018, Trump's "maximum pressure" policy had been extraordinarily successful, cutting the flow of money to Kim's coffers by about half. Then, the president changed course. That month, his administration did not go forward with sanctions on almost three dozen Chinese, Russian, and other entities that had been handling Kim Jong Un's cash.

The president, at the G-7 summit in Ottawa, just days before his historic meeting with Kim in Singapore on June 12, 2018, said he wanted to give Kim a "one-time shot" to disarm. Trump's policy, apparently, was to create such a favorable environment that Kim would feel secure enough to give up his most destructive weapons.

Since that time, there have been scattered American designations of Kim's money launderers for sanctions violations, but for the most part the administration has relaxed enforcement. Because the Kim family changes front companies all the time, the failure to designate new fronts has allowed Pyongyang to hollow out sanctions. Similarly, the Trump administration, after designating Bank of Dandong a "primary money laundering concern" on June 29, 2017, pursuant to the Patriot Act, has allowed other Chinese banks to handle Kim's cash without interference. The secretary of state, Mike Pompeo, said often in 2018 that the U.S. was maintaining pressure on Kim, but his words were misleading.

Moreover, the Trump administration has pursued other Kim-friendly policies, like scaling back or ending exercises between U.S. and South Korean forces even though the North has continued its drills, most notably its four-month-long Winter Training Cycle. Perhaps most important, Trump has, through inappropriately laudatory comments, provided legitimization of Kim Jong Un and his horrific regime.

Moon's view, at least as expressed in public, is that Kim Jong Un has already gone too far to turn back. "Now, North Korea's decision to relinquish its nuclear program has been officialized to a degree that not even those within North Korea can reverse," the South Korean president said in late September.

At the moment, Trump administration policy is based on a similar – but less heroic – assumption: Kim has made a strategic decision to give up his nuclear weapons and ballistic missiles so that his regime can enter the international order. If Moon and Trump are correct, then alliance partners Seoul and Washington will stay on the same page.

Yet Kim clearly has not made that fundamental decision. Since the first Trump-Kim summit, the North Koreans have been upgrading both their nuclear weapons facilities, especially the Yongbyon complex, and missile sites, including the Yeongjeo-dong base. The North also has been increasing production of fissile material.

None of this is a violation of the June 12 Joint Statement, which merely states that "the DPRK commits to work toward complete

denuclearization of the Korean peninsula."
Yet its intransigence and hostility since the
summit are indications that Kim has not
decided to disarm. So too are Pyongyang's
various pronouncements that it would not
abandon its "treasured sword of justice," code
for its most destructive weapons.

In these circumstances, American policy
will almost surely return to real pressure and
more threats of "fire and fury." When that
happens, the gap between American and
South Korean policies could become a gulf.
Then the alliance could finally break, because
Washington can tolerate only so much South
Korean "balancing."

SOUTH KOREA'S LAST PRESIDENT?

"Moon, the son of North Korean refugees, is
likely to be the last South Korean president
with any kind of sentimental aspiration for a
reunified Korean peninsula," writes S. Nathan
Park in the *Atlantic*. Perhaps that's why some
now think there is a "once in 1,000 years oppor-
tunity for both Koreas to agree to peace."

That grand-sounding assessment may not be too far off. Now there are two Korean leaders who look absolutely determined to find a common unification formula. Kim Jong Un, like his two predecessors, wants to take over the South, and Moon Jae-in looks like he is trying to help him do it. In any event, the South Korean leader is not a firm believer in freedom, democracy, or human rights, and he does not particularly like America.

Kim Jong Un, as a result, apparently thinks he can achieve unification on his terms. After all, he has been talking about "final victory," North Korean lingo for taking over the South. Now, for the first time since the early days of the Korean War, that looks possible, perhaps even probable.

Moon Jae-in, the nineteenth president of the Republic of Korea, looks determined to be its last. Kim Jong Un, of course, is determined to make that a reality.

First American edition published in 2019 by Encounter Books, an activity of Encounter for Culture and Education, Inc., a nonprofit, tax exempt corporation.
Encounter Books website address: www.encounterbooks.com

Manufactured in the United States and printed on acid-free paper. The paper used in this publication meets the minimum requirements of ANSI / NISO Z39.48–1992 (R 1997) (*Permanence of Paper*).

FIRST AMERICAN EDITION

LIBRARY OF CONGRESS CATALOGING-IN-PUBLICATION DATA IS AVAILABLE

10 9 8 7 6 5 4 3 2 1